HANNINGTONS

A brief history 1808-2001

BRIGHTON'S LEADING HOUSE

Sidonie Bond

S.B. Publications

Dedicated to Kate and Tom Merrin, my daughter and son, for their encouragement, forbearance and assistance.

First published in 2002 by S B Publications
19 Grove Road, Seaford, East Sussex BN25 1TP
01323 893498
fax 01323 893860
sales@sbpublications.swinternet.co.uk

ISBN 185770 252 2

Typeset by JEM Editorial, Lewes
JEMedit@AOL.com

Printed by Tansleys Printers
19 Broad Street
Seaford
East Sussex BN25 1LS
01323 891019

Cover picture: *Old Hanningtons*, watercolour attributed
to Thomas Allorn, 1804-1872

CONTENTS

FOREWORD

*H*aving been born and brought up abroad, I knew very little about Hanningtons of Brighton until the Second World War when, as a young officer, I visited the shop to enquire about having a new uniform made. Although by then the firm had passed out of family control, I thought it would be nice to have a uniform bearing a label of the firm started by my great-great grandfather over a century previously. I was treated with great courtesy and the kindly head of the tailoring department told me, quite honestly, that I would probably do better by going to one of the other of the two regular suppliers of uniform, both of which had branches in Hove. On reading Sidonie Bond's narrative it is apparent to me that a high degree of courtesy, good service and honesty have been a feature of the firm throughout its long history, right up to the end.

Sidonie Bond has researched the start, the growth and the sad demise of Hanningtons of Brighton at depth, and I am sure that her fascinating findings will be of great interest not only to residents of Brighton, but to many others from further afield. She has presented a lot of facts in a very interesting and readable manner, and at the same time has provided much information about the changing customs and fashions over almost two centuries. She has also given enlightened accounts of the backgrounds and characters of those of the family who were involved in the business, and I am delighted to have been invited to write a foreword to her book. I am confident that it will give a great deal of pleasure to those who read it.

Michael Hannington

'I cannot imagine Brighton and Hove without this century-and-a-half-old store, fit to rank with the world's best. As Brighton simply would not be Brighton without it, here's to the next hundred-and-fifty years.' *Vivian Rowe, 1960*

INTRODUCTION

*A*n accidental series of events led to the compilation of this history of Hanningtons, Brighton's famous department store. I was committed to a final essay for my History of Art and Design course run by Brighton Museum and Art Gallery. I preferred to localise the subject matter and had already researched some of Brighton's architectural history and the changes for better or worse throughout the past centuries. The Art Gallery had purchased a painting, *Brighton Coach Office*, by Robert Dighton (1752-1814) – see page 33. I was curious to place this picture in its present day setting.

The two shops, Lambert and Howell, were easy to trace thanks to the library's local history section. I found myself standing opposite, outside Laura Ashley (the Stiles Horton Building) in Castle Square, looking across the road at Pressley the jeweller (Howells) with the corner of Hanningtons (the Coach House) at my left. Just out of the picture was 3 North Street, Smith Hannington's first shop. As I stood looking at the area, I realised it was that very week I had learnt that the store was to close, and so my essay was decided.

The history of Hanningtons spanned 193 years during which many changes had taken place to the building, not all creditable and at times confusing. How often throughout the years shoppers would lose their way trying to find a particular department in the store! It would be impossible to write only of the social trends and changing fashions in clothing and furnishing. My essay received 'a good review' and I was encouraged by my tutors to develop the story of Hanningtons into an interesting and informative read. I hope I have achieved this.

Sidonie Bond 2002

*Charles Hannington
(1734-1797)*

*Smith Hannington
(1784-1855)*

1
THE FIRST SHOP

Smith Hannington, founder of the Brighton store, was born in Shoreham in 1784. His father, Charles, a local brewer, was known as a man of super-human strength. There were many tales of his skill – one of a cart stuck in mud, which six men found impossible to move. Charles dismissed them, lifted the cart and freed it single-handedly. Stories of his ability to carry large barrels of ale continuously, without tiring, were legendary. Smith's mother was Mary Mepham, a well-born woman who may have descended from the family of Simon de Meopham, an Archbishop of Canterbury in the fourth century. The Hanningtons' first child was Charles Mepham, born in 1774, who trained as a solicitor. He was described in the diaries of Smith's grandson, James, as 'selfish, burdening his widowed mother and draining her of her slender purse'. Another son, Henry, born in 1776, died at the age of five.

Maybe, unlike his brother, Smith did not show an academic bent, or perhaps, after the expense of Mepham's studies, there was little finance left for Smith to do likewise.

Smith was apprenticed at fourteen to a drapery company in Brighton. It is possible his parents paid a premium and that Smith earned little or nothing for four years. Most apprentices at this time lived in and paid for their board and lodgings, but it is likely that Smith lived at home in Shoreham. The long working hours, up to eighty-five a week, plus his travelling, must have been strenuous and wearing. But his experience, training and later employment gave him the ambition and enthusiasm to set up in business independently.

When Smith was twenty-three it is said that an associate, deeply in debt, offered him the opportunity to buy 3 North Street. Another version of how Smith acquired the property is that he had invested in the building and when his associate –

the owner –died he left it to Smith. Either way it was a stroke of luck for young Smith Hannington. His confidence and ambition are clearly demonstrated in press announcements of the shop's opening.

From the *Brighton Herald* of July 25, 1808:

Linen Drapery, Mercery, Haberdashery, and Hosiery.
NO 3 NORTH STREET.

SMITH HANNINGTON begs leave most respectfully to inform the Inhabitants and Visitants of Brighton, and its vicinity, that he has taken the above mentioned shop (late Tamplin and James) and intends OPENING on MONDAY NEXT, July 25th. with a new and elegant Assortment of Goods in the above branches, which will be sold for Ready Money at such unusual low Prices, as, he trusts, will secure the future Patronage and Support of those who may be pleased to confer on him their favours.

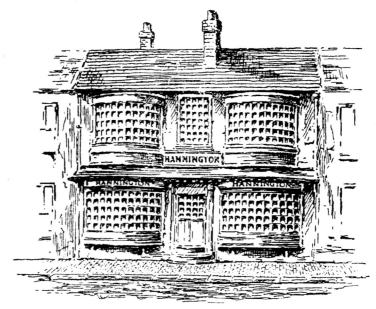

Smith Hannington's first shop at 3 North Street

A similar announcement appeared in *The Sussex Weekly Advertiser* on August 1, 1808.

The shop was small – 30ft wide, 12ft deep, 14ft into the bays. Smith's knowledge of buying the best, of what his clientele desired, and the long hours he was prepared to work placed him on the pathway to success. His business served the upper and middle classes (at that time the lower classes rarely entered shops and bought mainly from markets and from pedlars), and his company policy of 'low prices for ready money' denied credit and kept his finances safe. Smith seldom closed his shop, unlike previous owners of the premises, the Constable brothers, who regularly posted notices on the door saying 'gone away for a few days'.

William and Daniel Constable had opened *their* store in 3 North Street in 1802 to sell draperies and 'gadgets'. The brothers famously promoted their business during the Feast of St Bartholomew (September 3 to 5) with a daring high wire act. Their stunt was the highlight of a festival of entertainment that included theatrical performances, exhibitions, displays of exotic animals, bands, games, competitions and stalls from the Steine to the Level. The Constables erected scaffolding and high wire from a point where St Peter's Church now stands to the maze in Ireland's Royal Pleasure Gardens north of the Level. Daniel attired himself in cream silk tights and gossamer wings, attached wheels and pulleys to his back and, waving flags, hooked himself to the wire and attempted to fly across the Level. Large crowds gathered to watch, but their cheers turned to jeers when Daniel became stuck, dangled for a moment and slowly descended.

When the Constables sold their shop to Smith Hannington's associate they went to America where they re-invented their flying device, and this was successfully used world-wide to rescue people from burning buildings and sinking ships.

The brothers returned to Brighton in 1841 and introduced the

The Age loading passengers and luggage at Castle Square for the run to London, 1829. At that time some thirty coaches a day plied between the capital and Brighton – traffic which brought prosperity to Smith Hannington's expanding store

latest form of photograph, the daguerreotype, in their studio, the Blue Room on Marine Parade.

In 1810 the Brighton Town Act was brought in to formalise growth of the town. It empowered 106 commissioners to appoint watchmen, beadles and constables 'to widen the streets by compulsory purchase'; provided for new pavements to be laid; ordered that no new shops should project over the pavements; and set out penalties for those who dumped rubbish in the streets, on the beaches or over the cliffs, and those who played games or committed nuisances in the streets.

George III had, by now, lapsed into 'senile dotage' and the Prince of Wales, the future George IV, assumed the mantle of Regent in 1811. The king, 'effectively imprisoned', was unable to contradict his son. Regency Brighton had arrived.

2

EXPANSION AND INVESTMENTS

*S*mith Hannington had chosen the ideal time in history and the perfect location in Brighton to launch his business. The population was expanding rapidly and visitors flocked to the fashionable resort. This was at first due to the sea-water cure promoted by Dr Richard Russell of Lewes, in the mid-eighteenth century. Society was attracted to the former fishing village of Brighthelmstone to 'take the waters'. A generation later, in 1783, the Prince of Wales came to stay as a guest of the Duke of Cumberland in a house (previously owned by Russell) on the site now occupied by the Albion Hotel. The Prince was captivated by all he saw and conquered by the town's charms, and shortly afterwards he began work on his fabulous seaside palace. The arrival of the Prince's court in Brighton inspired the elegant terraces, squares and gardens that still characterise the town – and that guaranteed an ongoing increase in trade for Smith Hannington. His shop was adjacent to the principal coach office at 1 North Street and close to the Royal Pavilion.

In 1809 a contemporary diarist, HR Attree, wrote:

In truth, Castle Square and the half of North Street, may be said to be the Bond-street of Brighton; and in the latter there are as many well contrived and furnished shops as those of Bond-street of the Metropolis.

Smith married Elizabeth Staker in that same year, and in 1816 he received the Royal Warrant – a just reward for his hard work and enterprise. Also in 1816 his mother died, and with his inheritance and his wife's dowry he was able to buy the freeholds and leaseholds of adjacent properties. These were:

1824, 4 North Street (which later became the carpet and furniture warehouse)
1839, 2 North Street
1843, 1-8 Brighton Place (sublet to tradesmen not in competition to himself and later used for staff lodgings)
1845, 1 North Street, the coach office (which was leased to Treachers Stationers and Library)
1847, Pear Tree House, Market Street, leased to a Mrs Reid.

Smith's son Charles then entered the business and by 1862 he had acquired the lease of 5 North Street.

The Hannington empire was now growing rapidly and profitably, helped not least by the arrival of the railway in 1841 and a period of great expansion in Brighton and Hove. Popular items among Smith's expanding stock list included trousseaux, complete outfits for the colonies and mourning dress (at that time worn for a year or more on the death of a close relative).

In 1846 Hanningtons established a funeral and undertaking business at 42 East Street that continued until the 1960s. The Hanningtons name in the funeral business has been retained and continues in Hove.

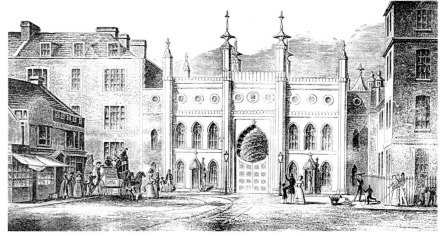

South gate of The Royal Pavilion, and coach office, c1830

Hanningtons' receipts from the 1820s

Smith Hannington never ceased in his hard work and was described by his grandson, James, as a man who never wanted a holiday but never thought anyone else wanted one either. He was living in North Street when he died in 1855 at the age of seventy, leaving a widow Elizabeth and his surviving children, Charles and Martha. Elizabeth had borne six children; Mary, the first, died aged eighteen in 1829; Anna, born in 1816, died at the age of nine; John, born 1817, died in 1849; Lydia, born 1820, died in 1846.

In an obituary in the *Brighton Herald* on July 28, Smith was described as:

> *Venerable, with a kindly looking face and his snow white locks . . . a large capitalist who used many opportunities of aiding others and did so with no little constraint.*

In 1832 Hanningtons apprentices signed a contract which read:

His master he shall faithfully serve, his secrets keep, his lawful commands everywhere gladly do. He shall do no damage to his faithful master, he shall not waste goods of his said master nor lend them unlawfully to any. He shall not commit fornication, nor contract matrimony within the said term (six years). He shall not play at cards or dice tables, shall not haunt taverns or playhouses, nor absent himself from his said master's service day or night unlawfully.

13

3

THE NEXT GENERATION

*C*harles Smith Hannington inherited the business after his father's death in 1855. Writing in his diary, James tells of his enterprising father leaving school at thirteen 'having read more than I ever did for my degree!'

In 1847 Charles Smith bought a large estate at Hurstpierpoint where the family made its new home, although the Hanningtons' houses at 18 Brunswick Terrace in Hove, and 11 Russell Crescent, Brighton, were retained. His son, Charles Henry, described the new country home in his memoirs.

I recall the grounds of the rambling mansion of St. George's, Hurstpierpoint, which seem to have impressed me earlier than my day or night nursery. They were grounds to enchant a child; the gorgeous carpet-bedding of the formal garden; the large lily-pond with its life-size statues and its mysterious depths where the great goldfishes lurked; the walled bee garden with the strawberry beds and the raspberry canes and the wall fruit and the great fig trees. But above all there was the little lake, with its island and its inlets and its rustic bridge, the boat-house for the punt and the dinghy, and a real small two-masted yacht (with the keel cut away) anchored in the middle to serve as a weather-vane. Then there were all the glass houses, the orchard house where oranges were growing, the vineries, the tropical house and the different flower houses and last of all the mushroom house, deep underground like a real cave, to be visited by the dim light of a tallow candle. There were Summer-houses of various shapes and sizes and a brick-built and thatched roofed croquet house bowered in masses of roses, honeysuckle and clematis. There were

Charles Smith Hannington's Hurstpierpoint mansion

vast Araucarias, deodars and many other rare and beautiful trees, and great shrubberies where a child could be hid and watch the kingfishers, the swans and the many water-fowls on the lakes. From the grounds the 'long walk' led down past the laundry and the paddocks, under the arches of roses and borders of large arbutus and other flowering shrubs, to another part which crossed the orchard of 'Little Park' Farm Houses . . . It passed the upper Carp-pond and then crossed the lower pond by a long bridge and entered the 'Wilderness', a large wood through which winding pathways had been cut and the streams crossed by rustic bridges. There was a shooting box with a kitchen where shooting lunches were served and where we gathered primroses, bluebells and anemones in the Spring time. There were many other delightful spots on the estate of 1000 acres, kept up regardless of expense and a very paradise for a child.

Describing the house, Charles Henry wrote:

The old house . . . was a veritable museum of beautiful

pictures, rare furniture, choice china, bronzes and sculpture, wonderful carpets and old silk damask hangings; the rooms fragrant with masses of hot-house flowers. Every Country in Europe had contributed to its furnishing, and the sack of the Tuileries in 1871 had provided some especially beautiful specimens. On the left of the entrance hall was the music room with a full-sized Church organ in mahogany case with gilded pipes; and at the other end of the long apartment was a fernery

Charles Smith Hannington (1813-1881)

with two fountains and a vast variety of ferns collected by James Hannington who was a noted botanist. Another door led into the Louis Seize drawing room, and then across a wide passage into the library with its huge oak book cases and rows of ancient tomes and splendid specimens of the book-binder's art. A large Ante-room divided the library from the great dining room, a panelled room with fine oil paintings of old sailing ships, and large enough for Mess dinners when the officers of my father's Brigade of Volunteer Artillery dined with their Hon.

Elizabeth Clarke Hannington (1815-1872)

16

The lily pond with two-masted 'yacht'

Colonel. The band under Bandmaster Lanfried, who as a trumpeter had sounded the Charge of the Light Brigade at Balaklava, used to play during dinner.

In 1852 Colonel Charles Smith Hannington acquired the large estate of neighbouring Little Park to expand and enclose his land. He was a man who liked to have his own way and was intolerant of those who crossed him. Canon Borrer, the rector of Hurstpierpoint's parish church, with whom he disagreed, was told by Charles 'not to come the High Priest over me' and caused Charles to leave the Church of England. He built the non-conformist Little Park Chapel, facing west instead of the traditional east, in the grounds of his estate. This became known as the Chapel of St George and in 1867, having reconciled his differences with the established church, Charles Smith rejoined the Church of England and the chapel was licensed. Eight years later his son, James, was appointed Curate-in-Charge (James was followed as curate by Henry Montgomery, whose son became Field Marshal Bernard Montgomery of Alamein).

The chapel, now without its bell turret and its once beautiful stained glass windows, remains, and two services are held there each month.

The Hannington children ran wild in the grounds of St George's and occasionally their mischievous activities had to be checked by a taste of the birch. In 1859 James lost a thumb when a home-made explosive meant to blow up a wasps' nest went off too soon.

By 1860 Charles Smith Hannington was wealthy and independent. He liked to mix with the nobility and to live in grand style. He bought a large yacht, *Zelia* (200 tons), which was launched with great ceremony by his daughter Mary. So imposing was the vessel that it was once mistaken for the Royal Yacht. Later Charles commissioned the building of a steam yacht, the *Iola*. He was frequently at Ryde when the Royal Family was in residence on the Isle of Wight and he entertained the court aboard his yacht. Charles Henry described in his diaries how the family travelled to Southampton for the yachting season. A train was assembled at Hassocks Gate, as Hasssocks was then known, with a first class carriage for the family and a second class one for staff. Horse carriages and traps were loaded on to a wagon with the luggage and provisions.

Charles Smith had eight surviving children, five sons and two daughters by his first wife, Elizabeth Clarke, and another son, Charles Henry, by his second wife, Blanche Caroline Goold. Of the sons, Samuel joined him in the business at the age of fifteen and later James started work in the Counting House, also at the age of fifteen.

James went on to join the first Sussex Volunteers, rising to the rank of major. A lover of botany, geology and mineralogy, he was totally unsuited to business life and in 1868 he left to study divinity at St Mary's Hall, Oxford. On September 25, 1875, James became curate of St George's Chapel on the family estate at Hurstpierpoint. In 1877 he married Blanche Hankin-Turvin. Five years later James left England for missionary work in East Africa. The parting with family and parishioners was, apparently 'most painful'. Farmers closed their market early so that they would not miss his farewell words. In 1884 James was consecrated as the first Bishop of Equatorial East Africa.

Charles's yacht, Zelia

On July 23, 1885, James set out to explore a new and shorter route through Masai country to Lake Victoria, with a caravan 226-strong. But illness, hostile natives and food shortages caused delays and postponements. The expedition rested at Kiva Sundu and restarted on October 12, with a reduced company of fifty. James's last diary entry was on the morning of October 29, when he reached Lake Victoria, 170 miles from Kiva Sundu. Mwanga, the Kabaka of Uganda, alarmed by this unusual approach by a white man, ordered him to be seized, and James and all but four of his attendants were speared to death. Those who survived escaped and returned to base with the news of the Bishop's brutal murder.

A native of the time was reported as saying: 'The gun is the weapon for the white man and they know what charm to use to avoid the bullet – the spear is our weapon and the European has no charm against it.'

Bishop Hannington's remains, which were identified as his by a missing thumb, were perhaps initially buried near the site of his execution. On June 18, 1886 the foundation stone was laid for St Paul's Cathedral on Namirembe Hill, near Kampala. James's remains were recovered and interred here on the last day of 1892. The building, consecrated in James's memory in 1904, holds 4000 worshippers. James's Bible, diary and chalice are kept by the cathedral.

James, thirty-eight when he died, left his wife, Blanche, and four surviving children.

At home, Bishop Hannington Church was built as a memorial to the missionary bishop in Holmes Avenue, Hove. Money

Bishop James Hannington (1847-1885)

was raised locally and in 1934 the church hall was completed. The Reverend Gordon Guinness, the first incumbent, began services in the hall. The church's foundation stone was laid on November 26, 1938, by the Bishop of Chichester, George Bell, and present at the ceremony was James's son, the Reverend J Hannington.

The church, which is brick-built, was designed by Edward Maufe, architect of Guildford Cathedral, and is described as like Guildford on a smaller scale. It was consecrated on November 2, 1941.

Blanche Hannington (1846-1932)

4

GROWTH OF DEPARTMENT STORES

*C*harles Smith gained the freehold of 5 North Street in 1862 and he also bought a single-storey property at 171 North Street. He employed the architect William Russell to develop and expand his properties and create 'A Department Store'.

At that time, drapers' shops were expanding to become department stores naturally, as they had always maintained a diverse trade, catering for the needs of their clients during changing times. For example, Hanningtons provided a removal and storage service for people moving to the large new properties being built in Brighton and Hove during the second half of the nineteenth century. This led to a complete furnishing service that included curtains, floor coverings, furniture and household linens. Hanningtons also offered a furniture cleaning, repairing and re-upholstering service. The huge population explosion during the Victorian era was highly profitable for the ever-expanding Hannington family empire.

France claimed to have had the first department store with the opening, in 1850, of Bon Marche – but was this so? There were Kendal Milne in Manchester in 1837, Bainbridge in Newcastle in 1841 and Peter Robinson in Oxford Street, London, in 1833. And in London Road, Brighton, the Brighton Co-Operative Society opened its store in 1828.

The spending power of the people reflected the huge increase in trading. By 1861, clerical occupations had increased by 400 per cent and average wages were £5-10 a month. A small house could be rented for £35 a year and a grand house with stabling and servants' quarters for 300 guineas a year.

In 1860 Charles Smith Hannington formed the First Sussex Volunteer Regiment with his staff and others. They practised on Saturday afternoons and it was at this time that he reduced the

Hanningtons, Market Street, 1857, the Golden Fleece, left

shop hours and instituted early closing and half days.

The Hannington family appears to have cared exceptionally well for the recreation and welfare of their staff. From 1866 the family home, Little Park at Hurstpierpoint, was used annually for a sports day. The entrance fee was sixpence and staff were encouraged to compete for generous prizes of five shillings and half-a-crown. Cricket matches also took place in the season between, for instance, the Establishment and the Counting House, and Married Men and Single Men.

Charles Smith died in 1881 and his son Samuel took charge. In 1882 Samuel acquired 41 East Street, where millinery, lace and fancy dress were sold, and also 42 East Street, where the undertaking business was established.

A property in Lewes Road, next to The Ship pub, was bought for a carpet beating and cleaning service. The machinery used, exclusive to Hanningtons, was the most advanced of its time for removing dust and moth eggs. Carpets – which were not fitted in those days – were collected by Hanningtons and taken away 'for a few days' before being returned 'completely refreshed and made to look like new'. This was to become

Inside the carpet-cleaning workshop

East Street shops acquired by Hanningtons in the 1880s

another highly profitable part of the business.

In 1883 the telephone was installed for orders and enquiries, the number being Brighton 7. Today, there are many arguments regarding the erection of mobile phone antennae masts; in the 1880s when Samuel Hannington wanted to instal the telephone he, too, had to fight with neighbours and leaseholders for permission to erect telephone poles and cables.

Samuel and his family remained in Hurstpierpoint and became local benefactors, providing a trust to help poor parishioners, giving land and assisting with the running costs of the village school and of St Christopher's Home for the Aged.

5

HANNINGTONS' PEOPLE

*I*n comparison with contemporary wages, Hanningtons paid well above average. Between 1876 and 1878, sales staff were earning up to £7 10s a month, while seniors earned £9 3s 4d a month. Junior staff started on £30-40 a year, and apprentices (aged fourteen to sixteen), some with a premium paid by their families, earned nothing during their two to three year apprenticeship. These young people were required to change the window displays at dawn each morning. Workshop staff – and there were almost 100 needlewomen employed in the mid 1800s – were paid a little more than sales staff, a workshop supervisor at that time receiving the peak amount of £10 a month.

In 1872 Charles Smith Hannington had been approached by a deputation led by David Sharp and William Hilton. They said, in their petition:

> We have hesitated to express our wishes on any previous occasion, because we thought the time had not arrived when we could conscientiously ask such a boon as the suspension of business at two o'clock on Saturdays; but we feel now that its adoption is only a question of a short time, and that if you were willing to grant so great a boon it would be a bond of closer and more loving union betwixt you and ourselves, and would preclude the possibility of that ill feeling which is too often engendered by concessions unwillingly wrung from employers after bitter and angry agitation.

The petition was successful, Charles Smith 'conceded the boon' and hoped the move would meet with 'the cordial approval and support of the Public'. 'Every exertion will be

In his 1885 Guide to Brighton, W E Nash wrote, of Hanningtons:

This is the largest business house in Brighton, employing over 300 hands, and embracing all the branches and ramifications of complete house furnishing . . .
All the shop assistants dine upon the premises, and the arrangements for their comfort and recreation are of the most elaborate character, including library, billiard and reading room &c., for the sterner sex; and the utmost comforts for the young ladies including pianoforte, library, &c.

used, not only to prevent any inconvenience arising from such an arrangement,' he said.

Even so, most of the staff worked up to sixty hours a week. It is curious that, later – from 1910 until 1914 – there was actually a drop in wages, the highest being less than £6 a month. Perhaps this was because of the further shortening of working hours and the increase in salaries paid to trainees and junior staff.

Living-in was expected and, unlike in other stores, board and lodging was free. In 1881 thirty-two male employees lived in nine cottages in Brighton Place, and fifteen female staff in rooms at the top of 42 East Street. There were no married quarters. Lodgings usually had to be vacated by 8.30am on weekdays and 10.30am on Sundays; the live-in staff were not allowed to return until about 7pm. But Samuel, concerned about his staff's moral well-being and the possibility of them being lured into the local taverns, changed the rules and allowed access and provided meals on Sundays. Everyone had to be in by 11pm. Men were treated to an annual outing in July – but women had no outings.

From 1880 department managers were given more responsibility and buyers began travelling abroad to purchase stock – to France, for instance, to buy patterns of the new fashions and to seek the latest fabrics and trimmings.

Long and loyal service reaped the benefit of promotion and good salaries.

Discussion of wage increases was discouraged and secrecy among the staff was imperative. The explanation for this, a condition which continued well into the twentieth century, was that the Hannington family would listen sympathetically, in private, to requests for pay rises, but those who were successful were told not to discuss their new wages for fear of upsetting those whose requests had been turned down. Another benefit, for both living-in and living-out staff, was free meals, unlike in other companies where the cost was often deducted from wages.

By 1896 the Staff Library and Recreational Club was being run by the staff for the staff instead of by the store, and a fee of two shillings a quarter was paid. Accounts for beer and spirits are documented. The library was considered quite luxurious. Most books had a religious and moral theme but the committee of eight chosen staff members was encouraged and allowed to consider requests entered in the proposition book. Papers and periodicals were also available.

However, men and women were segregated with a ladies-only sitting room and a men-only reading room. Even selection of books was at different times for men and women. This club remained in some form or other until the 1960s when The Lanes extension took place and the club premises was lost.

In 1896 electric lighting was introduced to twenty-four departments in the store, and to all of the Hanningtons buildings in 1897. Until then the store had been lit by gas.

Trade and expansion continued and many buildings which the Hanningtons had purchased leasehold became available freehold and were added to the property portfolio.

A tea room for shoppers on the first floor was opened in 1897, later a restaurant for 'ladies who lunch'.

Hanningtons' prestigious North Street-West Street corner property was leased to Treacher's Library between 1845 and 1924

6

COMPETITION AND ADVERTISING

*I*n 1896 Hanningtons department store was successfully floated as a public company with Samuel and his son Charles as managing director and deputy. From the beginning of the 1900s Hanningtons had faced competition from other new stores in Brighton and Hove such as Knight and Wakefield at 50 Western Road (KW remains embossed on the frontage between elegant towers), and Hills of Hove at Palmeira Square, which supplied superior goods for the rich residents of Hove.

In 1898 Sharman, a milliners, outfitters and drapers, had opened in Western House, a magnificent gothic building at the junction of Western Road and Montpelier Road – designed as a private home in 1822-1825 by Amon Wilds and Charles Busby. The Sharman shop was replaced by Plummer Roddis (later Debenhams) which opened in 1921.

In line with the practice at these other stores, by 1918 the female staff of Hanningtons were required to wear uniforms. The fabric was bought in the store and the women and girls either made the uniforms themselves or paid a dressmaker. Each year the uniform colour changed, which proved expensive for the staff.

Samuel died in 1926 and his half brother, Charles Henry (son of Charles Smith and his second wife, Blanche), inherited a major part of the property at Hurstpierpoint. Charles Henry had taken other professional paths including the military, farming and the law. He wrote later:

> When Samuel Hannington died in 1926, I had to take over the management of the land which had been consistently bled for 45 yrs. It was a difficult and ungrateful task, as the charges on it were heavy and

everything needed renewing when my Mother died. I had to start selling all that was saleable, and on the demise of Bishop Hannington's widow I put down enough ready money to wind up the Hannington Will Trust and as a legatee took over the remains of the Estate, some 700 acres as a frozen asset.

Charles Henry had no heirs.

Samuel's son, Charles Smith, remained a major shareholder of the company. It is said he 'frittered away' a considerable amount of money and that he drank heavily. Charles Smith had one child, a daughter, Dorothy, who inherited his shares and became the last Hannington on the board.

The property had been constantly changing and expanding as leases expired. Finance was needed to keep up with the times and for modernisation. The 1890s had seen the acquisition of the second floor of 53 Market Street, 6 and 7 North Street, 1 Market Street and 2 Pavilion Dormitories on the east side of New Road, close to North Street. In 1896 new shop fronts had been put in at 1 and 2 North Street, and in 1898 plate glass windows were fitted at 2, 3, 4 and 5 North Street. In 1901 the frontage to 1-12 North Street was made uniform. In 1903 the freehold of 43 East Street was returned to Hanningtons.

Numbers 6, 7, 8 and 9 North Street remained let to Barclays Bank – number 8 until 1923, when Hanningtons converted this area, including 11 and 12 North Street, for shop use between 1924 and 1926. The glass skylights and well here are a past memory of banking days. Numbers 13 and 14 were leased to J Lyons tea rooms but returned to Hanningtons in 1954.

By 1900 newspaper advertising was playing a significant role in the marketing of the store, and for £10 a year Hanningtons could rent the side board of a motor bus to display its advertisement. In the same year a 77ft billboard advertising the store was erected beside the railway line a quarter of a mile before the station.

In 1890 the first advertising calendar, and diaries for special customers, were produced. Samuel Hannington published

Drapers, Silk Mercers, Outfitters and General House Furnishers,
2, 3, 4, 5, 171 & 172, NORTH STREET; 41 & 42, EAST STREET, BRIGHTON.

S. HANNINGTON & SON'S ANNUAL SUMMER SALE
Will Commence on **MONDAY, JUNE** 27th, 1887.

Annual summer sale advertisement, 1887

Early 1900s postcard carrying details of a sale on the back

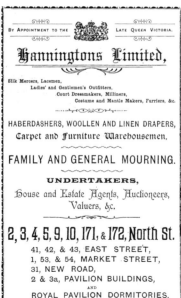

Above, advertisement on a motor bus outside the Connaught Hotel in Hove Street, 1904
Left, turn-of-the-century newspaper advertisement

postcards illustrating the store and advertising the selection of wares and future sales, and Hanningtons also advertised the latest fashions in periodicals such as *The Brighton Season*.

Hanningtons catered for the 'middle market' by providing ready-to-wear as well as personal dressmaking and tailoring services. Corsetry – previously executed by a corset surgeon or

*Brighton Coach Office by Robert Dighton (1752-1814);
the coach office is seen on the corner of East Street and
North Street and the road opposite is Pavilion Buildings*

The Market Lane façade during the store's 'blue' period

THE MODERN NOTE
BIZARRE WARE DINNER SERVICES

Beautiful in its austere severity. Pottery made with no corners to harbour dust, no incisions to retain grease. Decorative colour features introduced to give an added touch of distinction.

SOLOMONS SEAL PATTERN

Dinner Set comprising 26 pieces for 6 persons . . £2 . 15 . 6
54 pieces for 12 persons . . £5 . 5 . 0

STAMFORD PATTERN
Dinner Service comprising
26 pieces for 6 persons . £2 . 15 . 6
54 pieces for 12 persons . £5 . 5 . 0

Other makes of Dinner Sets include Coalport, Doulton, Losol, Minton, Wedgwood and Booth's Silicon.

Large Showroom for
KITCHEN EARTHENWARE
PYREX OVENWARE, DENBY AND APILCO FIREPROOF CORNISH KITCHENWARE ETC.

HANNINGTONS   BRIGHTON

Advertisement for Clarice Cliffe Bizarre ware, 1920

*St George's at Hurstpierpoint, which was converted
into eighteen luxury flats in 2002*

*Little Park, Hurstpierpoint, which took over
from St George's as the family's country home*

*Chapel of
St George
in the
grounds
of the
family
home at
Hurstpier-
point*

*Hanningtons'
doormat now
welcomes
visitors to the
author's
seafront home*

Hanningtons' Waists were 'stoutly reinforced at armholes, amply provided with buttons and equipped with the Hunkins Patent Pin-tube for attaching hose supporters'. For boys and girls the price was from 1/11d to 4/6d and for Edwardian ladies, 5/11d

corsetiere in the privacy of the customer's home – could now be fitted and bought in the store thanks to revolutionary new garments from America.

Early in the twentieth century the store became the local agent for Burberry and a series of Burberry ads reflected the popularity of motoring and the emergence of the suffragettes.

In the years before World War One there were some notable advances in advertisement, design and layout, significantly the influence of Art Nouveau and the replacement of drawings by photographs of real models.

In the 1910s the first advertisement offering deferred payments appeared. It promised customers complete discretion. It had taken just more than 100 years for Hanningtons to offer

Above, Burberry's 1910 topcoat, The Motor, had a quilted lining 'of Eiderdown, Swansdown or Cotton Wool throughout', and was 'the epitome of lightness and genial warmth' Left, 'a 'Superfine Seal Musquash Trimmed Beaver', 140 guineas, from the 1920 season

FURNISH OUT of INCOME

HANNINGTONS' SCHEME OF DEFERRED PAYMENTS

VARIED AND INSISTENT AS ARE THE CLAIMS ON CAPITAL TO-DAY it becomes quite obvious that it is not always convenient to convert one's cash balance into a furnished home. The man of business feels he should give prior claim to the demands of business ; the newly married, to reserves against the " rainy day," ; and the man of varied interests prefers to leave investments undisturbed.

An extended credit system has been devised to meet the needs of such and similar cases, providing for payment over a period of years if need be, under conditions that have been cleared of the stigma attaching to outworn systems of " hire purchase."

Hanningtons have approached this aspect of modern life with a view to removing many of the difficulties in the path of the would-be furnisher, and have devised a method, which enables the complete furnishing of a home, or the purchase of a single article, to be paid for by convenient instalments.

Hanningtons have no intention of making these matters unduly public. They do not desire to enter into a field of activities where terms are of prime importance and furnishings of secondary consequence. They intend to maintain their reputation for the excellence of their furniture, leaving the matter of terms to the individual circumstances of the customer.

HANNINGTONS' SCHEME

All arrangements made under the Scheme are treated as strictly confidential, and the Scheme is entirely financed by this firm.

Advertisement for Hanningtons' deferred payment scheme

39

credit, Smith Hannington, the founder, believing it to be the downfall of good business practice.

But now there was competition from newer department stores in Brighton and Hove. Vokins, Maples, the Army and Navy Stores and Hills of Hove had attracted customers to their linen, furniture, household and fashion departments, although Hanningtons was favoured for its tradition of personal service, for its size, the luxurious decor and its ever-increasing selection of goods.

Moving ahead of the times, Hanningtons countered the attractions of rival businesses by offering space in its store to companies specialising in china and glass, exclusive fabrics and travel goods. Commissions on sales paid the rents. This was an early example of the practice of placing shops and boutiques within a shop that is widely practised today.

A 'Smart Gown' advertised by Hanningtons for the 1923-1924 season – the fashionable lady as country milkmaid look

40

7

THE NEW STORE

*L*eases had expired and been returned to Hanningtons by 1924 – most particularly that of the corner shop leased by Treacher's Stationers and Library – enabling the business to expand further. After major works and renovations, the refurbished store was opened in 1926. The furniture department was laid out in room settings, an innovation at the time for Brighton, although undoubtedly copied from major London and Paris stores.

The increasing population, their needs and spending power, justified the expansion and diversification of Hanningtons, which included a new gramophone department, and a china

Building the extension where Treacher's had been

and glass department. It was said that you could shop as well at Hanningtons as anywhere in the world.

A new costumes and gowns department was advertised as 'echoing fashionable Paris', where the latest creations could be faithfully copied by Hanningtons' expert dressmakers 'and offered at most reasonable prices'. In the department devoted to 'Dressing Gowns and Tea Frocks' were, the advertisements promised, 'dainty silk negligees, cosy bed jackets and gowns of lambswool, crepe de chine and silk Zenana'.

Bedroom furniture was displayed in two extensive showrooms and Hanningtons claimed to make a special study of 'fitted wardrobes for both men and women'.

In the new youth department there were 'charming well-made ready-to-wear Coats, Costumes and Frocks in all sizes for the girl of every age'. School clothes were made to measure for girls by workers who were 'used to the slim figures and unexpected angularities of youth'.

An illustrated guide to the relaunched store, a pamphlet

Hanningtons' children's fashion parade, Grand Hotel, 1934

Completion of the extension, 1926

called *Progress*, waxed lyrical about 'the fascination of the Hat' and the store's well-stocked millinery department. Here, too, hats could be designed and made to order in Hanningtons' own workrooms. Among the other delights to be found at Hanningtons, *Progress* pointed out, were its excellent fur department, which had its own cold store for customers' furs in summer time, and its unrivalled perfumery department.

As the store expanded it increased its telephone service from one to five lines and thirty-two extensions to cope with the hoped-for increase in trade.

Lingerie at the foot of the store's elegant curving stair

8

THE FORTIES AND FIFTIES

*T*he Second World War had a devastating effect on Hanningtons, as it had on most other businesses. Staff were called-up and rationing, clothing coupons and, later, 'Utility' goods, were introduced.

Hanningtons also suffered from the bombing of Brighton. On the evening of Friday, November 29, 1940, German bombers blanketed the town centre with incendiaries, followed by a number of high explosive bombs. East Street was worst hit, and Hanningtons suffered serious damage to its corner shop at 1 North Street. Fortunately there were no injuries or fatalities in Brighton that night, despite the ferocity of the raid.

A popular local figure during the war years was flower lady

Bomb damage to the East Street-North Street corner shop

Harriet Gunn, whose favourite pitch was the doorway of one of Hanningtons' East Street shops. She told a wartime *Evening Argus* reporter: 'I ain't going to move from my corner for Hitler nor anybody else. You just got to die once my duck. I'll be sitting here a long time after Hitler and his bunch are finished.' And so she was.

Two other well-known street characters were harpist Frederick Alexander, and violinist Joseph Marcantonio. In the years before the First World War they played to trippers taking paddle-steamer rides from the piers. When, in the early twenties, the musicians were turned off the streets by the council for busking, Samuel and Charles Hannington gave them permission to play in one of the store entrances, next to Harriet. This continued for many years until Harriet's death in 1949, when the two very elderly musicians played at her funeral. Harriet had sold flowers on Brighton streets for sixty-four years. Joseph died in 1958 and Alexander in 1963.

The post-war period was not a profitable time for Hanningtons. Competition, prices, staffing and updating the departments were costly. Rationing, particularly of

Flower seller Harriet Gunn

clothing, had affected trading. But there was a feeling of a better future. Prime Minister Harold Macmillan's 'We've never had it so good' was around the corner. Utility remained, but the New Look and contemporary design beckoned.

Hanningtons Motors, which provided garage services and

Frederick Alexander and Joseph Marcantonio in East Street

limousine hire, became a successful part of the business in the 1950s. The Van Alen building on Marine Parade now occupies the site.

Customer/staff relationships changed with the arrival of the half century. No longer would the shop walker guide the customer to a comfortable seat and introduce a member of the sales staff to attend upon his or her needs, or offer a gentleman an ash tray while his wife tried on the latest fashions. Once there had been time for a lady to discuss the new trends, colours and trimmings, and catch up on the latest gossip with the sales assistant, but no longer.

One thing that didn't change until some years later was the cashier system that dated from the twenties. There was only one till in the store, and one cashier, who was installed in a booth on the ground floor with a shiny brass cash register. When goods were bought, an invoice was written out by the salesperson and taken to the cashier to be paid for and receipted. The receipt would then be returned to the department and the goods collected. Beside the cashier's booth was a vacuum tube for use when a certain amount of money had accumulated in the booth, or when more change was needed. A brass container was sucked away to the basement where accountancy staff dealt with the request, entered amounts in ledgers and placed cash in the safe. Only at sale times were extra tills brought into use, and then there were only another two.

Customers with accounts were able to avoid the time-consuming cashier system. Hanningtons' account customers considered themselves superior and privileged, and maybe they were, but staff who worked there during these years told how, sometimes, the system was abused.

One account customer, who was hardly ever seen in the store, used to send her chauffeur to collect a selection of gowns, coats or hats for her to try on at home. This was referred to as 'appro' – meaning on approval. On one occasion staff remember her requesting six black hats so that she could choose one for a funeral. A week later all six were returned as not suitable. No doubt at least one of them had attended the funeral.

Another customer visited the store only infrequently, but when she did it was made into a grand occasion when goods would

The store's old-fashioned cashier system became the victim of a scam in the 1950s when a number of furs were supplied to a Mr Habers, who had a furrier business in Hove. A fake receipt was issued and the cashier was bypassed. It was only when Mr Habers checked to find what had been sold and what commission was owing to Hanningtons that the store discovered fur coats were missing and no records of any sales. The scandal was hushed up to save the reputation of the store, and those involved were sacked.

be laid out for her to view, with the staff standing by. It was her habit to point and say 'yes' or 'no' to the items on display. The 'yes' goods were then delivered to her on 'appro', but mostly they were returned with a note saying that these were not the items she had picked out.

These recollections come from Rosalie Butler, Marion Brewer and David Langley, who worked in the store in the 1950s. All said they felt privileged to work at Hanningtons in an era when it was considered 'an honour' to be employed there.

Rosalie, aged sixteen, became a junior sales assistant in the gown department in 1959. Her seniors were strict and never addressed by their first names. She remembers Rene Garbutt, chief seamstress, who wore her tape measure around her neck like a chain of office. It was reputed there was always a bottle of gin in her workroom. Miss Garbutt was extremely courteous to the customers, but sometimes appeared 'a little over-tired' or was found asleep in her workroom. Though Rosalie was in fear of her, she said Miss Garbutt had 'a heart of gold' and she remembered her with fondness.

Shirley Harris and Ann Langley, Hanningtons office clerks, out for a breath of fresh air in the Pavilion grounds, 1953

It was exciting when the stars visited Hanningtons, Rosalie said. Among those she remembered were Vera Lynn, Flora Robson, Vivien Leigh, Minnie Caldwell and Dora Bryan. Dora, who lived in Brighton, was most often to be found in the household department with her friend, Gracie Fields, looking at kitchen equipment.

Marion started as a ledger clerk in the basement in 1952 and her early memories are of a high stool, a sloping desk and a small window looking out on Market Street where she could see only feet passing by. Later she was chosen to man the till on the fashion floor at sales time, and was noticed by a fashion buyer who promoted her from the basement to her office on the first floor. Marion achieved fame for herself and for the store when she won the title of Miss She at Butlins' Ocean Hotel in 1956. Marion left Hanningtons to start a family, but

Marion Brewer, aged twenty, voted Miss She of 1956. Marion wore fashions from Hanningtons

returned in 1976 to work part-time for the next ten years as a telephone switchboard operator.

David Langley started work at Hanningtons when he was a little older than the others, having completed his National Service. As a sales assistant in Fabrics, he sold Harris Tweed, Tootal cotton, French Jacqmar and embroidered silks. At sales time he used to buy silk remnants and have these made into waistcoats for himself. In the fifties sales staff earned threepence in the pound commission, which in departments with a high turnover could amount to a considerable sum. In later years the commission was scrapped in favour of a bonus scheme.

David had fond memories of senior salesman Freddy Bleach, who had fought in the Battle of Jutland, and who was an accomplished lecturer on fabrics in local colleges. Freddy lived in an old cottage at Rodmell where he had a spinning wheel and where he dressed in a smock spun from his own wool. At the store's Christmas party, Freddy entertained staff by playing his zither.

Once a year staff were treated to a formal dinner dance at the Winter Gardens in the Metropole Hotel. Romance blossomed for Marion and David at one of the dances and soon, after a courtship in the staff canteen, they were married.

Rosalie and Marion met again in later years when both went to work for Legal and General, housed in what had been the store's depository, and next to the Hanningtons undertakers in Montefiore Road, Hove.

For some three years in the 1950s one of the most popular attractions at Hanningtons was a large fountain in the centre of the store, but it was removed when local lads persistently deposited soap powder in it, causing an overflow of suds that soaked the carpet and the customers. Was this the beginning of the new wave about to swamp Brighton – the era of the Mods and Rockers?

Sportswear in the 'fifties was more heavy, formal woollens than jeans and tees

9

SWINGING IN THE SIXTIES

*I*n the early sixties Fitzroy, Robinson and Partners was commissioned to extend the Brighton Lanes. The property owners were a consortium consisting of Hanningtons and the Church Commissioners. Brighton Corporation set aside the usual building regulations, making it possible for the project to take place. The scheme included the loss of the Lady Huntingdon Church in North Street, but it was believed to be in disrepair at the time. The project was a success and received the Premier Award of the Civic Trust in 1966. Flats were built above independent shops in the new Brighton Square, which was in the concrete brutalism style of the decade.

The last member of the Hannington family to remain on the board was Dorothy, who died in 1966. Dorothy, who had never married, left her shares to the Royal Sussex County Hospital and The London Hospital. A member of the family said that this was not surprising as the great loves of Dorothy's life were doctors and specialists, 'her main topics of conversation being her various illnesses, complaints and symptoms'.

The staff who were there at that time speak of a bleak and unhappy period. 'It was like losing one's parents; there did not seem

Brighton Square

A fashion show at Hanningtons in the 1960s

to be anyone to take our problems to,' said one. Dorothy's
bequest stipulated that the staff would always to be taken care
of. The store was donated to the hospitals in the form of a
charitable trust, but this caused considerable difficulties in the
running of a commercial business, and in 1969 the decision was

taken to sell Hanningtons. The two major contenders were a property company called South Bank Estates and the Fraser Group. The trust was concerned that South Bank was interested only in the property value and might close the store. Director Charles Hunnisett promised that the store would stay open for at least twenty years under South Bank and, unlike Fraser, which would bring its own staff to run the store, South Bank would retain existing staff.

In 1969, Hanningtons was bought by South Bank for £1,005,000. Charles Hunnisett became chairman of the board, and on his death in 1982 his place was taken by his son Derek.

During this time the depository and the removal business were sold and some shops were disposed of.

Part of the North Street façade in the 1960s

10
BEGINNING OF THE END

*F*or Hanningtons, the 1970s were innovative with ongoing improvements in the layout and decoration of the store. A major and successful addition was the opening of an in-store branch of Hatchards, the London bookshop, on September 1, 1978. The launch celebrations included book signings by authors Jilly Cooper and Clement Freud, and among guests were Lord Longford and David Attenborough. The bookstore was opened by Edna Healey, who signed her own book, *Angela Burdett Coutts*.

In 1978 Charles Hunnisett, who had previously donated £250,000 to the Royal Sussex County Hospital for a body scanner (unveiled by his friend, Earl Mountbatten), gave

Derek Hunnisett and his sister Patricia Kemball present a cheque for £3,000 to Phill Merry for an Argus Christmas Appeal

WINDOW DISPLAYS OF THE SEVENTIES

Bikinis and leisure wear from Xelbarden

The out-of-Africa look from Van Heusen

INTERIORS FROM THE SEVENTIES

The store's hair and beauty salon

Display of table linen and blankets

Never showy, a display of jewellery and watches

A leisurely way to choose wallpapers and fabrics

another £100,000 to the hospital. In 1979 Charles received the OBE for his charity work.

Derek, his son, continued his father's good works. He became a member of the Brighton Health Committee, and was president of the Sussex branch of St John Ambulance. He donated a considerable sum every year on behalf of Hanningtons to the *Evening Argus's* Christmas Appeal. In the town, Derek became known as 'Mr Charity'.

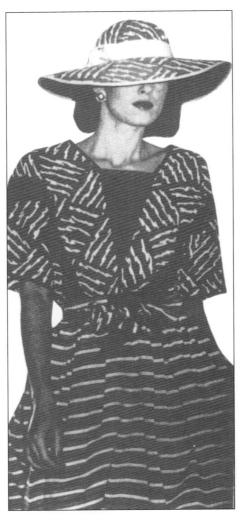

A Gina Donova cotton dress from 1985, priced at £159; the matching hat cost £59.95

In 1980 Hanningtons began publishing a store newsletter, which welcomed new staff, ran sponsored slimming and dancing marathons to raise money for the Charles Hunnisett scanner unit at the Royal Sussex County Hospital, and celebrated births and marriages. It offered low cost day trips and holidays abroad for staff and their families. It was a happy and social time for the store and those who worked in it, with dances and popular events such as the annual pantomime put on by the Hannington Players.

In 1984 Derek Hunnisett paid personally for a feasibility study to expand the Sussex County by 1,000 extra beds. The cost of the works was estimated at £40 million, but the expansion was never realised.

Disaster struck Hanningtons in the early hours of Wednesday, April 9, 1986, when a fire started in the Taverna Sorrento at the rear of the store. It spread rapidly throughout the carpet and television/audio departments. More than sixty firemen fought the blaze and 20ft flames could be seen rising from the building. Other parts of the store were saved and soon it was business as usual with the novelty, for Hanningtons, of a 'fire sale'. Arson was proved and a woman, believed to be a dissatisfied customer of the restaurant, was arrested, charged and convicted.

Promotional events continued to attract customers. There were fashion shows, compéred by such celebrities as Nanette Newman, beauty evenings, previews and competitions. One of these was to find 'the prettiest legs in Sussex', the prize being tights and £50 to spend in the store.

A major improvement for both staff and customers was the first floor bridge built over Market Street in 1989 to link the main store with departments in East Street. In fact, the bridge linked fifty departments, leaving only the toy shop in Market Street, the Royal Worcester department at Regency Corner in Brighton Place, and the pen shop in North Street independent.

Early in the 1990s came the first hint of a new undercover shopping centre to replace the dated eyesore of Churchill Square; this, with the planned huge car parks, would be seriously detrimental to Hanningtons, for which customer parking was already a problem. But the store fought on, offering The Pier a two-storey space in the North Street frontage in 1993.

Another fire in the mid-1990s, this time in the linen department, disheartened the store, but a newly-painted and new entrance in North Street in 1996, followed by the refurbishment of the two entrances in Market Street, enhanced the exterior. Internally, a new escalator was followed by a new lift in August 1998, and by the Grand Lift in November 1999.

Early in 2001 Derek Hunnisett reluctantly considered an offer to sell Hanningtons. During the 1980s and 1990s other Brighton and Hove department stores had already closed – Vokins, Hills of Hove, the Army and Navy – all hit by the easy access of out-of-town malls, retail villages and designer discount emporia.

Derek could have employed a consultancy to deal with the redundancies of staff, but decided instead to organise this personally. He kept his promise to Dorothy Hannington. At least eighty per cent of Hanningtons' workers found jobs elsewhere, and familiar faces were soon seen in other town centre stores; they took with them that special Hanningtons' brand of service and courtesy.

Hanningtons announced the end would come on Saturday, June 30, 2001, and in the last few weeks the departments emptied as bargains were snapped up in a massive closing sale. Shop dummies, out-of-date diaries and even doormats were bought as souvenirs of Brighton's oldest and finest department store. As the *Argus* put it: '. . . shoppers were buying many of the last clothes, pieces of crockery and light fittings rather like bereaved relatives clearing out a loved one's home.'

The Scenic Lift 'incorporating the elegance of past traditions together with new modern techniques'

The bridge spanning Market Street, linking fifty of the store's departments, was opened in 1989

Now open: The Hanningtons 'Bridge'

One thing you won't find at Hanningtons anymore...

the weather.

The management and staff are pleased to announce the opening of the new Hanningtons 'Bridge' between the Men's Wear Department and the rest of the store.

Now, whatever you get at Hanningtons–from haberdashery to hi-fi equipment–you'll never get wet.

Hanningtons

Take a fresh look at Brighton's leading department store

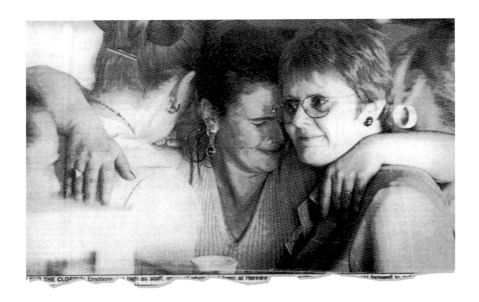

THE CLOSE: Emotions high as staff, ... when at Hanning... farewell to ...

TEARFUL FAREWELL: Customers and staff weep

673156

End of an era as the doors close

Cuttings from The Argus, July 2, 2001

YED UP: Store manager Trevor Guy locks up for the last time

.HE atmosphere felt like a .uneral party as staff sipped wine and reminisced while upbeat music masked the sombre mood.

As they remembered the tore's good old days it was as if hey were talking about ... nend

HANNINGTONS department store closed its doors for the last time on Saturday after almost 200 years in business in Brighton. LINSEY WYNTON spoke to shoppers and staff as they packed bags for the last

The Market Square façade of Hanningtons pictured in the year in which the store closed. The building with the clock is on the site of a stable block and carriage house where, once, huge doors opened to receive waggons bearing new stock, and to despatch vans carrying customers' orders. The buildings to the right used to be the store's depositories.The clock was stopped on the store's last day with the hands at noon. Derek Hunnisett and an assistant had removed the works and fixed the hands at twelve – enabling Hanningtons, like Cinderella perhaps, to find her Prince Charming.

11
MEMORIES

*A*t a final staff party on the store's last day friendships from years before were renewed, tears were shed and memories shared. Peter Godding, who started work in the menswear department in 1945, at fourteen shillings a week, remembered the time he created a window display featuring Burberry raincoats, and umbrellas. He said: 'When the Burberry representative saw this, he demanded the removal of the umbrellas immediately. "*Our* raincoats are waterproof, there's no need for umbrellas!" he declared.'

Peter recalled the formality of his early days, when the staff were called by their surnames and customers were addressed as 'sir' and 'madam'. Lowly apprentices could not speak to their managers unless spoken to first.

The store gave Peter a party to celebrate his fifty years at Hanningtons. He had expected the store to go on for ever.

Bernard Harding, the general manager for fifteen years until his retirement in 1995, said that although the shop had modernised over the years, it had kept its character and its traditional values.

'Without Hanningtons there is just going to be this big hole,' Gay Charles told the *Argus*. Gay had worked in Hanningtons for twenty-six years, in the jewellery and gift departments.

The property was bought by Regina Estates, an offshore company, for approximately £23,500,000. Planning permission was given for forty-six shop units on the ground floor.

Ten days after the final closure an auction held by Gorringes of Lewes took place in the central part of the store. A large crowd gathered for the sale of around 750 lots, and many familiar faces from the staff were present as well as several members of the Hannington family.

The sale of the Victorian mahogany wall clock, marked

Hanningtons' famous wall clock

'Hanningtons, Brighton' and estimated at £200-£300, drew a gasp from the crowd as the bidding reached £2,000. It went to Charles Boughton-Leigh, a member of the Hannington family.

An eleven-tread mahogany ladder, estimated at £50-£60, fetched £300. This ladder had been used to reach the winding mechanism of the clock in the tower facing on to Market Square.

Four family portraits (of Charles and Charles Smith Hannington), fetched £800, £700, £450 and £90. This last, badly holed, was bought by Chris Hannington, one of the younger members of the family.

The mahogany boardroom table and chairs sold for £5,300, and shop window mannequins went for around £20 each. One of the last lots was a wedding dress. This had been found boxed, covered in tissue, in a drawer. It had lain there, paid for, since the early 1960s, but was never collected. A costume collector paid £40 for it. A jilted bride, perhaps, or maybe a woman who changed her mind? It was an intriguing and sad end to a sad day.

But what happened to the Royal Warrant on the outside of the building? When did it disappear? What happened to the glass arcade, the entrance to the central ground floor of the building at approximately 5 North Street? Perhaps the original mosaic showing the Hanningtons emblem remains where the arcade used to be.

Sidonie Bond makes friends with a dummy

ABOUT THE AUTHOR

*S*idonie Bond was well-known for her appearances on television in the 1960s and 1970s. She was one of the original cast members in *Z Cars*, known for her catchphrase 'BD to Z Victor One'. She also appeared in *Steptoe and Son*, *'Til Death Us Do Part* and *The Avengers* among many others. Sidonie, a native of Liverpool, lives in Hove, and may be seen occasionally in a television cameo role.

Hanningtons' doormat now welcomes visitors to her seafront home.

Her daughter, Kate, is a television and film production manager, and co-owner of a model and promotion agency, and her son, Tom, is a television and film editor.

ACKNOWLEDGEMENTS

I am grateful to Dolly Winch and my course tutors for History of Art and Design at Brighton Museum and Art Gallery 2001.

I am greatly indebted to the Hannington family and especially to Michael Hannington for his generous assistance in making family history available to me, and to Chris Hannington for his help in providing photographs of family portraits.

Others who have helped include Wendy Walker at the County Records Office; staff at Brighton Local History Library; the Gunn family; Peter Tucket of Halifax Building Services, Pavilion Buildings (previously Stiles Horton and Ledger); Chris Horlock and his picture library; Derek Hunnisett and his PA Mona Smith; Jackie Benfield of Hanningtons; Peter Godding, Mark Dudeney for the picure on page 9, and many, many more.

SOURCES, REFERENCES AND BIBLIOGRAPHY

Berry, W Grinton: *Bishop Hannington*
Bishop, John George: *A Peep into the Past*
Butler, Michael J: *James Hannington of Hurstpierpoint*
Carter, Timothy: *The Encyclopedia of Brighton*
Chapman, Brigid: *Brighton in the Fifties*
Dawson, EC: *James Hannington*
Farrant, Sue: *Georgian Brighton*
Gray, James S: *Brighton between the Wars*
Hollindale, Eileen: *Old Brighton*
Nelson, Ian (ed): *Hurstpierpoint*
Pearce, Sally: *Department Stores*
Roles, John and Beevers, David: *A Pictorial Picture of Brighton*
Rowland, David: *The Brighton Blitz*
Sala, George Augustus: *Brighton as I have Known It*
Brighton Society 1900-1930
The Evening Argus and *The Argus, Brighton Herald, Brighton Gazette, Brighton and Hove Life.*